NINJA VS. MASTER CHEN

WRITTEN BY
CLAIRE SIPI

ALL IS NOT AS IT SEEMS

SEASON FOUR of NINJAGO™ : Masters of Spinjitzu sees the ninja scatter after the loss of their friend Zane. It takes an invitation to the Tournament of Elements to bring them back together. Join the ninja on their journey to a mysterious island. New dangers, new friends, and a big surprise await the ninja in a total of 14 LEGO® sets.

To find out more about this minifigure see p.7.

HOW TO USE THIS BOOK

This book is a guideto the LEGO® NINJAGO™ minifigures of Season 4. Learn all about the ninja's adventures in the Tournament of Elements and the skills they must develop in order to defeat their tricky opponents.

CONTENTS

MASTER CHEN
LEADER OF THE ANACONDRAI

Anacondrai skull and spine piece on head, with large purple snake around the skull

Distinctive face with mustache, goatee, and sideburns

DID YOU KNOW?
Master Chen used to train evil Garmadon and Clouse. He wanted to defeat Master Wu and for evil to rule all.

Tooth necklace

Robe with gold trim and snake scale patterns

NINJA FILE

LIKES: Wicked plans and complicated strategies
DISLIKES: Followers who are less intelligent
FRIENDS: Loyal Clouse
FOES: Non-Anacondrai
SKILLS: Tricking people
GEAR: Staff of Elements

SET NAME: Condrai Copter Attack, Enter the Serpent
SET NUMBER: 70746, 70749
YEAR: 2015

STAFF OF ELEMENTS
Chen's staff has the Power of Absorption—it takes the user's elemental power and stores it in the crystal orb. The elements can then be used by whoever holds it.

HOT-TEMPERED CHEN is a master of deception. He organizes the Tournament of Elements after Zane dies, as a guise to steal the powers of the Elemental Masters. With their powers he plans to perform a spell that will turn his followers into Anacondrai—and then he will destroy Ninjago Island!

PYTHOR

ANACONDRAI SURVIVOR REBORN

Long, curved neck, unique amongst Serpentine

Jagged, dark blade is more stylish and heavier than a regular dagger.

Head, body, and tail printing is now purple on a white background.

VILLAINS UNITE

Pythor is an excellent planner, and his sneaky and manipulative ways are just what Chen and the Overlord are looking for to help take over Ninjago Island. But first they must get past Master Garmadon!

THIS SNAKE LOOKS FAMILIAR!

After being inside the belly of the Great Devourer, Pythor has returned but has been bleached white. He wants to restore Serpentine dominance on Ninjago Island, so he allies with the Overlord to get revenge on the ninja.

TOURNAMENT KAI

FIERCE AND FIERY COMPETITOR

NINJA FILE

LIKES: Winning
DISLIKES: Secrets
FRIENDS: Skylor
FOES: Karlof, Chen
SKILLS: Building trust
GEAR: Double-edged
sword, scythe Jade Blade

SET NAME: Kai Drifter,
Jungle Trap, Dojo Showdown
SET NUMBER: 30293,
70752, 70756
YEAR: 2015

Golden scythe

Gold badge with
fire symbol

ROUND ONE

When Kai and Karlof go head to
head in the tournament arena,
both are desperate to win the
powerful Jade Blade weapon.
Karlof grabs the blade in his
metal fist, but Kai removes the
fist and eliminates the Master
of Metal from the competition.

DID YOU KNOW?

Kai is the only ninja
to wield two types of Jade
Blade; one resembles a
two-edged sword, the
other resembles
a scythe.

DRESSED IN THE SLEEVELESS ROBES
given to him by Chen, Kai is ready to enter
the Tournament of Elements. The robe is
light—ideal for ninja parkour battle moves—
but has a padded chest plate for protection.
Kai is quick to enter the competition—not
stopping to think about Chen's motives.

TOURNAMENT COLE

TRICKED, THEN TRAPPED

NINJA FILE

LIKES: Reuniting with friends
DISLIKES: Mysterious trapdoors leading to prison, meals involving noodles
FRIENDS: Zane
FOES: Chen's henchmen
SKILLS: Escaping jail
GEAR: Scythe Jade Blade

SET NAME: Lava Falls
SET NUMBER: 70753
YEAR: 2015

Matching black bandana to disguise face

Scythe Jade Blade

Ninja gi decorated with chest strap shows the elemental symbols of Kai, Cole, Jay, and Lloyd.

NOODLE PRISON

Despite Cole's competence, he loses in the tournament. Chen's henchmen kidnap him and put him in a cell in the underground dungeons. His elemental powers are taken from him and he is set to work in the Noodle Factory!

ARMED WITH A SCYTHE JADE BLADE, and all in black, Cole looks as serious as ever. With planned moves and strategic thinking, Cole combines his weapon skills and strength to show the competition what he is made of. However, he will need more than new robes to get out of Chen's trap!

TOURNAMENT JAY

UNLUCKY IN LOVE

Spear
Jade
Blade

NINJA FILE

LIKES: Defeating evil
DISLIKES: Fighting with his friends
FRIENDS: Nya
FOES: Cole, Chen
SKILLS: Extreme speed and agility
GEAR: Spear Jade Blade

SET NAME: Jay Nano Mech, ElectroMech
SET NUMBER: 30292, 70754
YEAR: 2015

DID YOU KNOW?
The green bladed end of the Jade Blade weapons represents the head of a dragon.

LOVE FEUD
When Jay discovers that Cole has feelings for Nya too, he is angry with his friend. Chen takes advantage of this situation and pits the two ninja against each other in the tournament. From Chen's point of view, that takes two more ninja out of action.

Printing on leg piece shows robe sash and knee stripes

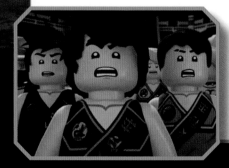

JAY'S NEW LIGHT AND FLEXIBLE tournament robe is the perfect outfit to show off his ninja speed and agility in the competition arena. His opponents had better watch out—wielding his spear Jade Blade, Jay is a formidable combatant, both in and out of the tournament arena.

TOURNAMENT LLOYD
JUNGLE-BOUND

NINJA FILE

LIKES: Visiting new places, such as jungles and islands
DISLIKES: Causing mishaps
FRIENDS: Fearless Kai
FOES: Master Chen
SKILLS: Helping others
GEAR: Flail Jade Blade

SET NAME: Jungle Raider
SET NUMBER: 70755
YEAR: 2015

Flail Jade Blade is a nunchuk-style weapon.

DID YOU KNOW?
The tournament uniform is only worn by Kai, Jay, Cole, and Lloyd. It is the first suit to not be worn by all five main ninja.

JUNGLE RAIDER

Lloyd's cool, green off-roader, with its large, spiked wheels, is the perfect vehicle to travel through the rough terrain of the jungle. Armed with front shooters, the Green Ninja can battle the evil Anacondrai tribe.

LIKE HIS FELLOW NINJA, Lloyd's new tournament robes reflect his powerful combatant status. When he finds himself as the only remaining competitor, and has to fight Master Chen, he has to use all his elemental powers to defeat the evil leader.

CLOUSE

MASTER CHEN'S SECOND-IN-COMMAND

NINJA FILE

LIKES: Spine-chilling spells
DISLIKES: The Cursed Realm
FRIENDS: Master Chen— he gives free noodles!
FOES: Garmadon
SKILLS: Sorcery
GEAR: The Book of Spells

SET NAME: Titanium Dragon
SET NUMBER: 70748
YEAR: 2015

DID YOU KNOW?

Clouse was one of the masterminds behind Chen's scheme to transform himself and his followers into Anacondrai.

Shuriken and snake fangs pattern on armor

Pike with four side blades

CHEN'S STUDENT

Clouse studied alongside young Garmadon under the training of Master Chen. When a duel broke out between the two students, Chen declared that the winner would become his right-hand man. Garmadon cheated and Clouse lost, for which Clouse never forgave him.

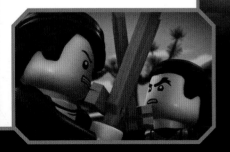

THE SINISTER, PURPLE-ROBED CLOUSE is a master of dark magic. He is a member of Chen's Anacondrai Army and proudly wears armor decorated with snake heads and fangs. Once Chen has collected all the elements, Clouse will use his evil dark magic to transform the warriors into Anacondrai.

SKYLOR
ELEMENTAL MASTER OF AMBER

Arrow and quiver

Japanese symbol represents the number 6—could Skylor become the sixth ninja?

Knee pads on leg piece

NINJA FILE

LIKES: The color red, mostly on Kai
DISLIKES: Devilish dads
FRIENDS: Kai
FOES: Anacondrai
SKILLS: Can absorb others' elemental powers
GEAR: Crossbow

SET NAME: Condrai Copter Attack
SET NUMBER: 70746
YEAR: 2015

DID YOU KNOW?

Skylor's mother was the previous Elemental Master of Amber, but no one knows what happened to her or where she has gone.

FAMILY TIES

During the tournament, it is revealed that Skylor is the daughter of Master Chen. When Skylor finds out how evil her father really is, she is torn between her daughterly loyalty towards him, and doing the right thing.

SKYLOR'S ROBES reflect her elemental power—Amber, or energy assimilation. With a simple touch, Skylor can absorb other powers and make use of them herself. A trained ninja and highly skilled with the bow and arrow, Skylor enters the Tournament of Elements. But can she be trusted?

KARLOF
ELEMENTAL MASTER OF METAL

NINJA FILE

LIKES: Shiny metals
DISLIKES: The thought of losing a fight
FRIENDS: Opponent Cole
FOES: Thieving Skylor
SKILLS: Power-packed punching, engineering
GEAR: Metallic fists

SET NAME: Dojo Showdown
SET NUMBER: 70756
YEAR: 2015

Samurai helmet

Shoulder pad armor with scabbard for two katana swords

Metal fists also worn by Gorillas in LEGO® Legends of Chima™ sets.

Silver metal body armor worn over black robe

FIRST ONE OUT
Karlof loses to Kai in the first round of the tournament when Kai craftily steals the Jade Blade from him. He is taken to a secret underground room where Chen drains his metal power. Defenseless, Karlof is then set to work in Chen's Noodle Factory.

WHAT BRUTISH KARLOF lacks in ninja fighting skills, he makes up for with his strength and stamina. He can turn his body into hard metal and his hands into giant metal fists—all of which enhances his punching power! Karlof comes from Metalonia, where he worked as a mechanic and an engineer.

GRIFFIN TURNER

ELEMENTAL MASTER OF SPEED

Dual-sided head (angry face without shades on reverse)

Griffin wields a sturdy staff as his weapon.

Aerodynamic kimono

NINJA FILE

LIKES: Winning races
DISLIKES: Delays
FRIENDS: Ninja
FOES: That cheater Chen
SKILLS: Awesome speed, kick-boxing
GEAR: Bo staff

SET NAME: Dojo Showdown
SET NUMBER: 70756
YEAR: 2015

DID YOU KNOW?

Griffin (along with Karlof and Skylor) is one of only three new Elemental Masters to appear in a LEGO set.

FASTER THAN FAST

Griffin likes to show off his elemental power and is extremely competitive. However, when he finds out what the evil Chen is really up to, he joins forces with the ninja.

BLINK AND YOU'LL MISS HIM! Griffin Turner can run at incredible speeds. In his red sunglasses and his kimono adapted for running, Griffin thinks he is one cool dude. He makes it through several rounds of the tournament, until he is tricked by Chen and has his powers drained.

EYEZOR

CHIEF ANACONDRAI WARRIOR

LIKES: Spreading fear

DISLIKES: Words—less talk, more action

FRIENDS: None. You can't beat up friends, can you?

FOES: Furious Kai

SKILLS: Bullying

GEAR: Anacondrai Blade

SET NAME: Condrai Copter Attack

SET NUMBER: 70746

YEAR: 2015

Mohawk hair piece instead of the snake helmet worn by all other army members

Leather vest with snake-head belt buckle and snake tooth necklace

Eyezor's Anacondrai Blade is a bone sword with jagged purple edges.

Silver "punk" chains and buckles printed on legs

CONDRAI COPTER CHASE!

Eyezor pursues Skylor through the jungle in the fearsome-looking Condrai Copter, with its adjustable wings for flight or attack mode. Firing missiles, he swoops down to drop a net over his victim.

Huge net shoots out from snake's mouth

VICIOUS EYEZOR is Chen's lead thug and a general in his Anacondrai army. His "punkish" look makes his victims quiver. Eyezor is always happy to do Chen's dirty work. He helps to run the Noodle Factory—he guards the enslaved workers and makes sure they work hard and don't escape.

ZUGU
ANACONDRAI GENERAL

Anacondrai snake skull helmet

Anacondrai Blade is the main weapon used by the Anacondrai Army.

NINJA FILE

LIKES: Food
DISLIKES: Prison breaks
FRIENDS: Eyezor
FOES: All of the prisoners
SKILLS: Sumo-wrestling
GEAR: Anacondrai Blade

SET NAME: Boulder Blaster, Enter the Serpent
SET NUMBER: 70747, 70749
YEAR: 2015

DID YOU KNOW?

Even though the warriors resemble Anacondrai, they need the venom of a true Anacondrai (such as Pythor) to finish the spell.

NOODLE-ICIOUS!

Zugu oversees production of the goods in the Noodle Factory, which are then shipped to Chen's Noodle House in Ninjago City. He watches the prisoners closely to make sure they don't eat any of the mouth-watering noodles!

THE BRUTISH ZUGU used to be a Sumo wrestler, before rising through the ranks of Master Chen's secret Anacondrai army to become one of his two generals. His bulk and strength make him a formidable opponent. He and Eyezor take great pleasure in frightening their prisoners.

KRAIT
ANACONDRAI HENCHMAN

NINJA FILE

LIKES: Serpents
DISLIKES: Being fooled by the ninja in disguise
FRIENDS: Kapau, Eyezor
FOES: Elemental Masters
SKILLS: Chopping logs
GEAR: Skull ax

SET NAME: Anacondrai Crusher, Jungle Trap, Krait
SET NUMBER: 70745, 70752, 901503
YEAR: 2015

Scar running over lips

Krait's torso and leg pieces are the same as on the Sleven minifigure.

Double-bladed bone ax

S-S-S-SECRET DISGUISE
The ninja want to find out what Chen is up to. So after capturing four of Chen's warriors, they disguise themselves in their outfits, make Anacondrai tattoos out of chocolate, and sneak into the secret Anacondrai temple.

KRAIT IS ONE OF MASTER CHEN'S muscled henchmen, dedicated to Chen's every villainous whim, and completely committed to the cause of the Anacondrai Army. He is a ruthless fighter. The ninja will have to use their powers and skills to the full to battle this ax-wielding brute.

KAPAU
AMBITIOUS ANACONDRAI

NINJA FILE

LIKES: Getting promoted
DISLIKES: Eyezor's jokes
FRIENDS: Chope
FOES: All of the ninja
SKILLS: Gaining power
GEAR: Double-headed fang dagger

SET NAME: Ninja DB X, Jungle Raider
SET NUMBER: 70750, 70755
YEAR: 2015

Bared fangs

Double-headed fang-shaped blade dagger

SABOTAGE
Chen orders his minions to sabotage the Elemental Masters' hunt for the Jade Blades. Kapau and his best buddy, Chope, happily rise to the task, albeit leaving a trail of chaos behind them!

WHAT HE LACKS in skills and talents, the vicious Kapau makes up for in ambition. When his dream of becoming one of Chen's chosen inner circle comes true, Kapau finds himself in way over his head. Not that this stops him trying to impress his master!

CHOP'RAI
CHOPE TRANSFORMED

NINJA FILE

LIKES: Slithering about
DISLIKES: Tough but slippery purple skin
FRIENDS: Kapu'rai
FOES: Master Wu—for organizing their defeat
SKILLS: Leading attacks
GEAR: Anacondrai Blade

SET NAME: Titanium Dragon, Ninja DB X
SET NUMBER: 70748, 70750
YEAR: 2015

Bone sword with sharp, jagged edges on the blade

Shoulder pad armor decorated with fang spikes

DID YOU KNOW?
The new Anacondrai are eventually banished to the Cursed Realm by some real Anacondrai ghosts, summoned by Master Wu.

TRANSFORMATION
Chope and Kapau complete the first part of the ritual of the ancient Anacondrai transformation spell from Clouse's spellbook in the Crystal Caves, where they are holding Skylor and Kai captive.

THE ANACONDRAI HAVE RETURNED!
Using Pythor's venom, the spell is completed and the warriors transform. Chope becomes the sly, blade-wielding serpent Chop'rai and his mission is to help Chen take over Ninjago. Will the Elemental Masters be able to defeat this new fearsome enemy?

KAPU'RAI
KAPAU TRANSFORMED

NINJA FILE

LIKES: His new tail
DISLIKES: Banishment
to the Cursed Realm
FRIENDS: Chop'rai
FOES: All of Wu's army
SKILLS: Guarding prisons
GEAR: Anacondrai Blade

SET NAME: Enter the
Serpent
SET NUMBER: 70749
YEAR: 2015

New head
and tail
pieces
identical to
Chop'rai's

DID YOU KNOW?

For the warriors'
transformation to be
permanent, they needed
the venom of a true
Anacondrai.

One red arm,
just like his
original form

Torso
decorated
with snake
scales

SOLDIER TO SERPENT

In his transformed serpent state,
Kapu'rai wears the same armor as
in his original warrior form.
However, when his legs
are replaced by his
huge new snake tail,
his battle robes get
torn and tattered.

WITH PYTHOR'S VENOM, Kapau is
able to achieve his dream and becomes
the terrifying armored snake, Kapu'rai.
With fangs bared, and tail-pieces on trend
again, Kapu'rai follows his master into
the final showdown with the Elemental
Masters in the Corridor of Elders.

JUNGLE KAI

GOING ON A SNAKE HUNT

DID YOU KNOW?
Once Kai starts believing in Skylor, he overcomes his trust issues and is able to unlock his elemental Fire Dragon.

NINJA FILE

LIKES: Playing hide and seek in the jungle
DISLIKES: Anyone who turns against their friends
FRIENDS: Skylor
FOES: Trickster Chen
SKILLS: Fooling Chen
GEAR: Golden swords

SET NAME: Anacondrai Crusher, Ninja DB X
SET NUMBER: 70745, 70750
YEAR: 2015

Bright red robes might not be best for hiding in the jungle!

Full-body gi with leather belt and chest pouch with fire emblem

Two kunai knives slot under leather scabbard chest strap

ELEMENTAL BOND
To Kai's overjoyed surprise, when he helps Skylor to escape from her father, she finally admits that she has feelings for him in return.

KAI AND HIS NINJA COMRADES must battle the loathsome Anacondrai in the thick jungle on Chen's deadly island. Luckily, Kai's new lightweight gi and zukin hood provide the perfect outfit for creeping stealthily through the undergrowth to ambush the Serpents.

JUNGLE COLE

ESCAPED PRISONER

NINJA FILE

LIKES: Blasting villains
DISLIKES: Returning enemies, such as Serpents
FRIENDS: Zane
FOES: Anacondrai prison guards
SKILLS: Piloting his Boulder Blaster
GEAR: Katanas, dagger

SET NAME: Boulder Blaster
SET NUMBER: 70747
YEAR: 2015

Ninja zukin showing Cole's elemental symbol

DID YOU KNOW?
Chen's new Anacondrai Army hides out deep in the jungle. The ninja must follow the soldiers there to defeat them.

Arrowhead knife slots into leather scabbard chest strap

Leather kneepads

PRISON BREAKOUT
In his roto jet Boulder Blaster, Cole finally escapes from the Noodle Factory prison. He uses the eight-missile spring-loaded rapid shooter to blast through the walls and fly past the Anacondrai guards.

EVENTS ON CHEN'S ISLAND reveal Cole's inner strengths and his progression towards achieving true ninja awareness and spirit. Dressed in his new jungle battle attire, Cole is more determined than ever to rid Ninjago Island of this latest Serpent evil, whatever the cost to himself.

JUNGLE JAY

STUCK IN A TRAP

NINJA FILE

LIKES: Saving his friends
DISLIKES: Serpent traps
FRIENDS: Karlof
FOES: Sleven
SKILLS: Executing escape plans with swagger
GEAR: Golden sai

SET NAME: Enter the Serpent
SET NUMBER: 70749
YEAR: 2015

One of two golden sai

Full-body gi with leather belt and chest pouch with lightning emblem

DID YOU KNOW?

In the NINJAGO™ TV series, Jay is imprisoned in an underground part of the Anacondrai Temple.

DOWN AND OUT?

The Anacondrai are holding Jay captive in their temple deep in the jungle. Can the ninja dodge the spring-loaded shooters in the stairs, the poison balls, and the hidden trapdoors to rescue their friend?

THE JUNGLE IS TREACHEROUS, even for the speedy and inventive Master of Lightning. Jay's face is disguised by his jungle zukin and he is armed with two sai and two knives, but he will still need all of his creative and stealthy ninja skills to avoid the hidden Serpent traps.

JUNGLE LLOYD

MAP READER

Leather scabbard for two golden katana swords

Flame torch

Map with directions to Anacondrai temple

SPELLBOUND!

Lloyd will need all of his powers to battle giant Serpents, find his way to the jungle temple and stop Chen using the spell to transform his followers into Anacondrai. His map will show him the way...

GREEN NINJA LLOYD is kitted out in the perfect color for jungle adventures. It is his mission to stop more dark magic. Equipped with a flame torch, a map, weapons, and wearing his special jungle robes—which offer excellent camouflage amongst the trees—Lloyd can creep up on his slippery enemy!

NYA
MASTER OF DISGUISE

NINJA FILE

LIKES: Surprise attacks
DISLIKES: Going undercover
FRIENDS: Fellow adventurer, Dareth
FOES: Chen
SKILLS: Fooling everyone with disguises and stealth
GEAR: Black katanas

SET NAME: Ninja DB X
SET NUMBER: 70750
YEAR: 2015

Samurai helmet with gold ornamental spiked crest

Face guard for protection and to hide identity

Nya's alternative samurai robe, and body armor is green with gold flames and a phoenix emblem.

KABUKI SPY
Resourceful Nya is a master of stealth and disguise. Dressed as a theatrical Kabuki girl, she sneaks into Chen's palace to find out what he is up to and to make contact with the ninja.

ON THE RUN FROM CHEN, his minions, and their Anacondrai transformation spell, Nya dons her fearsome-looking samurai armor and escapes into the jungle to find the ninja and warn them about Chen's evil plans. Leaving a fake trail of footprints, Nya eludes the enemy!

AUTO-PILOT ROBOT

DB X ROBOT DRIVER

Small blue head has golden binocular piece for eyes.

Gray pistol pieces used for arms

NINJA FILE

LIKES: Being useful
DISLIKES: Attacks on his home
FRIENDS: Nya
FOES: Chop'rai and Kapu'rai
SKILLS: Smoothly piloting the DBX in battles
GEAR: Ninja DBX

SET NAME: Ninja DBX
SET NUMBER: 70750
YEAR: 2015

Black skeleton pieces used for legs

ROBO UPGRADES

Nya is a talented mechanic. She built the D.B. Express (DBX), the ninja's mobile base complete with the auto-pilot robot and a cloaking device to alter the vehicle's appearance.

AUTO IS THE AUTO-PILOT ROBOT of the ninja's D.B. Express (DBX) vehicle. He can be activated to aid the driver in precarious situations. Taking control of the wheel in the front seat, he slides the driver into the back seat, freeing them up to fire missiles at the pursuing enemy.

TITANIUM ZANE

ICE NINJA REBUILT

Ninja zukin is a headwrap showing Zane's elemental symbol.

Titanium shoulder pad armor with scabbard for two katana swords

Two shurikens slot under titanium belt

NINJA FILE

LIKES: Embracing his new powers

DISLIKES: Fearing death

FRIENDS: Titanium Dragon

FOES: Clouse

SKILLS: Unleashing the Titanium Dragon

GEAR: Golden sai, katanas

SET NAME: Titanium Dragon

SET NUMBER: 70748

YEAR: 2015

TWICE TITANIUM

The new improved Titanium Zane has a dual-sided head with two Nindroid faces. One shows a happy, metallic robot face with blue eyes, whilst the other shows a serious Zane with a protective blue visor and robotic eyepiece.

UNKNOWN TO THE OTHER NINJA, when Zane was attacked by the Golden Master, he wasn't completely destroyed. A digital part remained, and Zane was able to rebuild himself as the Titanium Ninja. Dressed in cool titanium armor, Zane is shinier than ever, and ready to rejoin the ninja.

TITANIUM DRAGON

ZANE'S ELEMENTAL DRAGON

DID YOU KNOW?

The Titanium Dragon is the second Ninjago dragon with a brick-built head, the first being the Nindroid Mech Dragon.

NINJA FILE

LIKES: Making Zane proud
DISLIKES: Losing a battle
FRIENDS: Titanium Zane
FOES: Anacondrai
SKILLS: Freezing the enemy
GEAR: Armored body

SET NAME: Titanium Dragon
SET NUMBER: 70748
YEAR: 2015

Opening mouth with sharp teeth

Posable wings, legs, and tail

NIGHTMARE CREATURE!

The Titanium Dragon first appears to Zane in a nightmare. It is symbolic of his inner doubts and fear of death. Once he overcomes these fears, he is able to conjure the dragon at will and control it in reality.

THIS MONSTROUS DRAGON is a fearsome battle creature. Its huge body is covered in combat-scarred armored plates and spikes. It has sharp fangs and claws, and a spiked whip-like tail. Once Zane accepts that he is no longer just the Ice Ninja, he is able to control the beast.

Project Editor Emma Grange
Senior Designers Jo Connor, Mark Penfound
Editors Arushi Vats, Rosie Peet, Matt Jones,
Clare Millar
Designers Radhika Banerjee, Dimple Vohra,
Stefan Georgiou
Editorial Assistants Beth Davies
Pre-Production Producer Kavita Varma
Senior Producer Lloyd Robertson
Editorial Managers Paula Regan,
Chitra Subramanyam
Design Managers Guy Harvey, Neha Ahuja
Creative Manager Sarah Harland
Art Director Lisa Lanzarini
Publisher Julie Ferris
Publishing Director Simon Beecroft

First American Edition, 2016
Published in the United States by DK Publishing
345 Hudson Street, New York, New York 10014
DK, a Division of Penguin Random House LLC

Contains content previously published in LEGO®
NINJAGO™ *Character Encyclopedia Updated and Expanded
Edition* (2016)

001–298874–Jul/16

ACKNOWLEDGEMENTS
DK would like to thank Randi Sørensen, Martin Leighton Lindhart,
Paul Hansford, Madeline Boushie, Simon Lucas, Nicolaas Johan Bernardo
Vás, and Daniel McKenna at the LEGO Group, Gary Ombler for extra
photography, Andy Jones for extra editorial help, Sam Bartlett for
design assistance and Claire Sipi for her writing. For the original edition
of this book, DK would like to thank Shari Last, Julia March, Ruth Amos,
Lauren Rosier, Mark Richards, Jon Hall, Clive Savage,
Ron Stobbart, and Catherine Saunders.
www.LEGO.com

www.dk.com

A WORLD OF IDEAS:
SEE ALL THERE IS TO KNOW